Addition and subtraction
bumper book

Ages 5–7

$$6 + 4 = \boxed{10}$$

$$7 + 3 = \boxed{}$$

$$8 + 2 = \boxed{}$$

Brad Thompson

How to use this book

- Easy Learning bumper books help your child improve basic skills, build confidence and develop a love of learning.

- Find a quiet, comfortable place to work, away from distractions.

- Get into a routine of completing one or two bumper book pages with your child each day.

- At the end of each double page, ask your child to circle the star that matches how many questions they have completed:

Some = half or fewer   Most = more than half   All = all of the questions

- The progress certificate at the back of this book will help you and your child keep track of how many ⭐ have been circled.

- Encourage your child to work through all of the questions eventually, and praise them for completing the progress certificate.

Parent tip
Look out for tips on how to help your child learn.

- Ask your child to find and count the little mice that are hidden throughout this book.

- This will engage them with the pages of the book and get them interested in the activities.

(Don't count this one.)

Published by Collins
An imprint of HarperCollins*Publishers* Ltd
1 London Bridge Street
London SE1 9GF

Browse the complete Collins catalogue at collins.co.uk

© HarperCollins*Publishers* Ltd 2018

First published 2018

10 9 8 7 6 5

ISBN 9780008275464

The author asserts the moral right to be identified as the author of this work.

British Library Cataloguing in Publication Data.

A Catalogue record for this publication is available from the British Library.

All images and illustrations are © shutterstock.com and © HarperCollins*Publishers*

Author: Brad Thompson
Commissioning Editor: Michelle I'Anson
Project Manager: Rebecca Skinner
Cover Design: Sarah Duxbury
Text Design and Layout: Q2A Media
Production: Natalia Rebow
Printed by Martins the Printers

MIX
Paper from responsible source
FSC® C007454
FSC www.fsc.org

This book is produced from independently certified FSC™ paper to ensure responsible forest management.

For more information visit: www.harpercollins.co.uk/green

Contents

One more

1 Add 1 more bead to each string.

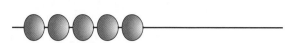

2 Add 1 more black spot to each of the ladybirds.
Write the total number of black spots in the box.

3 One child shouts out a number.
Their friend has to add 1 more.
Write the number that their friend should shout.

Parent tip
Play this game with your child. Give them a number and ask them to add one.

19

15

13

4 Draw a line to match each sum to the correct answer.

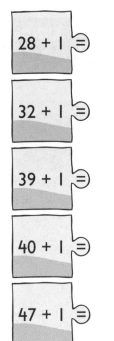

28 + 1 =

32 + 1 =

39 + 1 =

40 + 1 =

47 + 1 =

41

48

40

33

29

5 Add 1 more to each number.

48 ⟶ ☐   63 ⟶ ☐

57 ⟶ ☐   68 ⟶ ☐

59 ⟶ ☐   72 ⟶ ☐

6 Complete the sequences.
Start at the first number and
count on in 1s to find the
missing numbers.

65   66   67   68   69   ☐

73   74   ☐   76   77   78

77   78   79   80   81   ☐

86   ☐   88   89   90   91

94   95   96   97   ☐   99

How much did you do?   ## Questions 1–6

Circle the star
to show what
you have done.

 Some   Most   All

One less

1 For each group, find 1 less by crossing out 1 object.

1 less than 4 is ☐

1 less than 6 is ☐

1 less than 1 is ☐

1 less than 5 is ☐

2 Take away 1 apple from each tree.
Write the new number of apples in the box.

☐ ☐ ☐ ☐

3 There is a number written on each whiteboard.
Write the number that is 1 less.

Parent tip
Count out a number of objects for your child. Ask them to take one away. How many are there now?

19 ☐

15 ☐

17 ☐

13 ☐

4 Draw a line to match each subtraction to the correct answer.

20 – 1 =

35 – 1 =

38 – 1 =

44 – 1 =

47 – 1 =

37

43

19

34

46

---

5 Work out 1 less than each number.

☐ ← 50

☐ ← 57

☐ ← 61

☐ ← 64

☐ ← 73

☐ ← 78

---

6 Complete the sequences.
Start with the first number and count back in 1s to find the missing numbers.

65   64   63   62   61   ☐

23   22   ☐   20   19   18

47   46   45   44   43   ☐

16   ☐   14   13   12   11

78   77   76   75   ☐   73

How much did you do?   Questions 1–6

Circle the star to show what you have done.

 Some

 Most

 All

Number bonds for 5 and 10

Number bonds are really useful to know. They help you to add and subtract quickly!

1 Count the fingers on each hand and add them together.
Complete the number sentence.

$\boxed{4}$ + $\boxed{1}$ = $\boxed{}$

$\boxed{}$ + $\boxed{}$ = $\boxed{}$

$\boxed{}$ + $\boxed{}$ = $\boxed{}$

$\boxed{}$ + $\boxed{}$ = $\boxed{}$

Parent tip
Ask your child to add other combinations of numbers using their fingers.

2 Each star had 5 points.
Count how many points are broken. Then count how many points are left.
Complete the number sentence.

$\boxed{5}$ − $\boxed{}$ = $\boxed{}$

$\boxed{5}$ − $\boxed{}$ = $\boxed{}$

$\boxed{5}$ − $\boxed{}$ = $\boxed{}$

$\boxed{5}$ − $\boxed{}$ = $\boxed{}$

3 Fill in the missing numbers.

$1 + \boxed{} = 5$ $\boxed{} + 4 = 5$ $0 + \boxed{} = 5$

$5 − \boxed{} = 3$ $5 − \boxed{} = 1$ $\boxed{} − 4 = 1$

4 Count the spots on each side of the ladybird and add them together.
Write two different number sentences with the same answer for each ladybird.

7 + 3 = ☐   ☐ + ☐ = ☐   ☐ + ☐ = ☐

3 + 7 = ☐   ☐ + ☐ = ☐   ☐ + ☐ = ☐

5 Count how many fingers are down on each pair of hands.
Then count how many are left up.
Complete the number sentence.

10 − ☐ = ☐   10 − ☐ = ☐

10 − ☐ = ☐   10 − ☐ = ☐

6 Complete the number sentences.

1 + ☐ = 10   10 − ☐ = 3   ☐ + 4 = 10

10 − ☐ = 1   0 + ☐ = 10   ☐ − 4 = 6

Addition and subtraction within 10

Knowing addition and subtraction facts within 10 is very useful!

1 Add the dots on each side to find the total number on the domino.
Complete the number sentence.

3 + 4 = ☐

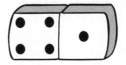

4 + 1 = ☐

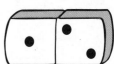

1 + 2 = ☐

6 + 3 = ☐

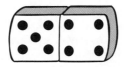

5 + 4 = ☐

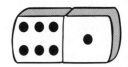

6 + 1 = ☐

2 Start at 10 on the number line.
Subtract the number by making the frog jump back in 1s.
Complete the number sentence.

| 0 | 1 | 2 | 3 | 4 | 5 | 6 | 7 | 8 | 9 | 10 |

10 − 5 = ☐

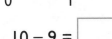

| 0 | 1 | 2 | 3 | 4 | 5 | 6 | 7 | 8 | 9 | 10 |

10 − 1 = ☐

| 0 | 1 | 2 | 3 | 4 | 5 | 6 | 7 | 8 | 9 | 10 |

10 − 9 = ☐

Parent tip
Help your child to add numbers by using a number line to count on if necessary.

3 Add the two blue numbers together.
Write the total on the top block.

| 5 | 4 | | 4 | 3 | | 3 | 0 | | 8 | 1 | | 0 | 7 |

4 Complete the number sentences.

$10 - 4 = \boxed{}$

$10 - 8 = \boxed{}$

$10 - 2 = \boxed{}$

$10 - 7 = \boxed{}$

$10 - 10 = \boxed{}$

$10 - 0 = \boxed{}$

5 See how quickly you can make your way around the race track by completing the calculations.

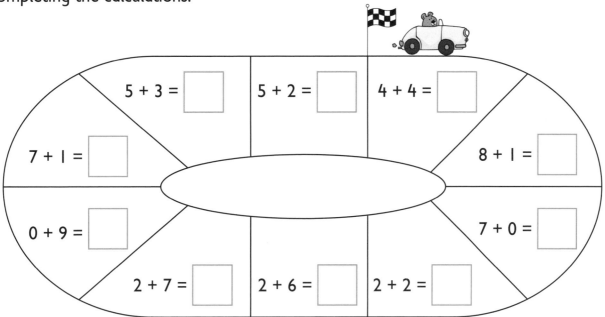

$5 + 3 = \boxed{}$ $5 + 2 = \boxed{}$ $4 + 4 = \boxed{}$

$7 + 1 = \boxed{}$ $8 + 1 = \boxed{}$

$0 + 9 = \boxed{}$ $7 + 0 = \boxed{}$

$2 + 7 = \boxed{}$ $2 + 6 = \boxed{}$ $2 + 2 = \boxed{}$

6 Work out the calculation on each part of the rocket. Use the code key to colour that part.

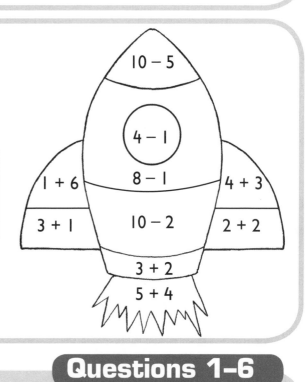

Code Key					
3	7	5	9	4	8
white	red	black	orange	green	blue

Number bonds for 20

1 The spots in each array are two different colours.
Complete the number sentence to show the number bonds to 20.

10 + ☐ = 20

1 + ☐ = 20

5 + ☐ = 20

15 + ☐ = 20

2 Draw a line from each fish to a bowl to make a total of 20.

 0
 2
 17
 16
 19

Parent tip
Play 'I say, you say!', e.g. 'I say 4, you say...?' Your child should give you the other number needed to make 5, 10 or 20.

 18
 20
 1
 3
 4

3 Draw a line from each jigsaw piece to another to make a total of 20.

 20
 8
 13
 11
 14

 6
 0
 9
 12
7

4 Complete the number sentences.

1 + ☐ = 20   15 + ☐ = 20   ☐ + 4 = 20

7 + ☐ = 20   14 + ☐ = 20   ☐ + 8 = 20

5 The two leaves on each flower add up to 20.
Write the missing numbers.

6 The top bar is 20.
The two bars under it make a
total of 20.
Write the missing numbers.

| 20 |
| 12 | |

| 20 |
| | 11 |

| 20 |
| 3 | |

| 20 |
| | 4 |

| 20 |
| 6 | |

| 20 |
| | 18 |

Addition and subtraction within 20

Learn and practise number facts up to 20. It will help with all areas of maths!

1 Add the numbers on each pair of socks.
Draw a line to match each pair to the correct basket.

 5 + 13
 8 + 8
 20 + 0
 13 + 4
 12 + 7
 14 + 1

 15
 16
 17
 18
 19
 20

2 Write in the missing numbers.

$15 - 4 = \boxed{}$ $11 - 8 = \boxed{}$ $19 - 2 = \boxed{}$

$18 - 7 = \boxed{}$ $15 - 10 = \boxed{}$ $13 - 0 = \boxed{}$

3 Each piece of string has a length cut off.
Complete the number sentences to show what is left.

14 cm

6 cm

$14 - \boxed{} = \boxed{}$

12 cm

9 cm

$12 - \boxed{} = \boxed{}$

Parent tip
Encourage your child to count on when subtracting, e.g. for 5 − 3, start at 3 and count on: 4, 5. That was 2!

17 cm

8 cm

$17 - \boxed{} = \boxed{}$

4 Add the coins in each purse together.
Write the total.

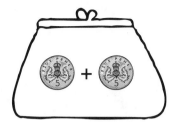 □ P

 □ P

 □ P

 □ P

5 Write the missing numbers.

$15 - \boxed{} = 9$　　$11 - \boxed{} = 4$　　$19 - \boxed{} = 11$

$12 - \boxed{} = 9$　　$14 - \boxed{} = 6$　　$17 - \boxed{} = 15$

6 In each group of triangles, some are grey and some are blue.
Complete the number sentences.

$\boxed{9} + \boxed{7} = \boxed{}$　　$\boxed{} + \boxed{} = \boxed{}$

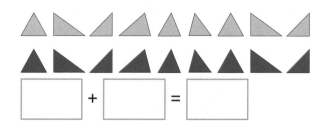

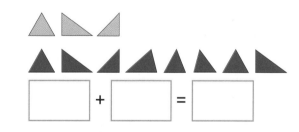

$\boxed{} + \boxed{} = \boxed{}$　　$\boxed{} + \boxed{} = \boxed{}$

How much did you do?　　Questions 1–6

Circle the star
to show what
you have done.

Some

Most

All

One-step problems

1 Tom has 15 football cards.
Riya has one more than Tom.

How many football cards does Riya have?

Parent tip
Encourage your child to act out the problem using objects!

[ ] football cards

2 Hiran has 20 marbles.
Kimberly has 3 less than Hiran.

How many marbles does Kimberly have?

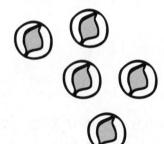

[ ] marbles

3 Jonathan has 13 sweets.
Ling has 2 sweets.

How many sweets do they have altogether?

[ ] sweets

4 Jane has 10 toy horses.
She gives 4 to her sister.

How many toy horses does Jane have left?

☐ toy horses

5 Beth picked 13 strawberries.
Chen picked 7 strawberries

How many strawberries did they pick altogether?

☐ strawberries

6 Laura has 18p.
She buys an apple for 11p.

How much money does she have left?

☐ p

How much did you do?   ## Questions 1-6

Circle the star
to show what
you have done.

 Some   Most   All

Counting on

1 Count the wheels on the bicycles 2 at a time.
Write the totals underneath.

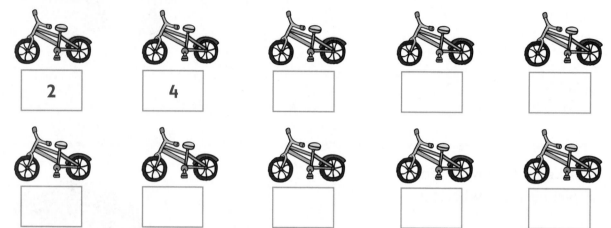

| 2 | 4 | | | |

2 Count the fingers on the gloves in 5s.
Write the totals underneath.

3 Count the leaves on the clover in 3s.
Write the totals underneath.

Parent tip
Encourage your child to count on out loud!

18

4 Count the beads on the abacuses in 10s.
Write the totals underneath.

5 Starting from 0, jump along the number line in 2s to 20.
Write how many jumps you made.

```
0   1   2   3   4   5   6   7   8   9   10  11  12  13  14  15  16  17  18  19  20
```

jumps of 2

Now jump along the number line in 5s to 30.

```
0  1  2  3  4  5  6  7  8  9  10 11 12 13 14 15 16 17 18 19 20 21 22 23 24 25 26 27 28 29 30
```

jumps of 5

6 There are 30 cricket balls.
Circle groups of 3 cricket balls. Write the number of groups in the box.

groups of 3

Now do the same for groups of 10.

groups of 10

How much did you do?   Questions 1–6

Circle the star
to show what
you have done.

☆ Some   ★ Most   ★ All

19

Counting back

1 Starting from 24, count back in 2s until you get to 0.
Write the next number in each part of the caterpillar.

24

2 Starting from 30, count back in 3s.
Drawing a circle around each number you land on.

1	2	3	4	5	6	7	8	9	10
11	12	13	14	15	16	17	18	19	20
21	22	23	24	25	26	27	28	29	30

Parent tip
Ask your child to count out the starting number using objects. Then keep taking away the given number.

3 Starting from 36, jump back in 2s along the number line.
Write how many jumps you make.

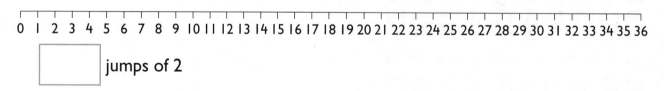

0 1 2 3 4 5 6 7 8 9 10 11 12 13 14 15 16 17 18 19 20 21 22 23 24 25 26 27 28 29 30 31 32 33 34 35 36

[ ] jumps of 2

Now do the same with jumps of 3.

0 1 2 3 4 5 6 7 8 9 10 11 12 13 14 15 16 17 18 19 20 21 22 23 24 25 26 27 28 29 30 31 32 33 34 35 36

[ ] jumps of 3

4 Start at the first number. Count back in 5s and fill in the missing numbers.

60 ☐ 50 45 ☐ 35 ☐ 25 20 15 ☐ ☐ 0

90 ☐ 80 75 70 65 60 ☐ 50 45 ☐ 35 30 25

5 Starting from 100,
count back in 10s.
Draw a circle around
each number you land on.

Do the same for 5s.
Draw a square around
each number you land on.

1	2	3	4	5	6	7	8	9	10
11	12	13	14	15	16	17	18	19	20
21	22	23	24	25	26	27	28	29	30
31	32	33	34	35	36	37	38	39	40
41	42	43	44	45	46	47	48	49	50
51	52	53	54	55	56	57	58	59	60
61	62	63	64	65	66	67	68	69	70
71	72	73	74	75	76	77	78	79	80
81	82	83	84	85	86	87	88	89	90
91	92	93	94	95	96	97	98	99	100

6 Starting at 100, count
back in 10s to find your
way through the maze.

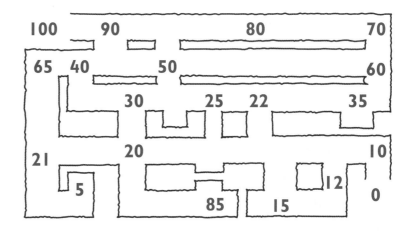

Partitioning 2-digit numbers

One way to add or subtract numbers is to break them up into tens and ones. This is called partitioning.

1 Partition these numbers into tens and ones.
Fill in the missing numbers.

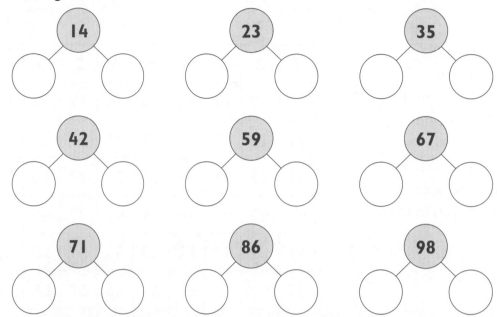

2 Start with the 2-digit number.
Take away the ones to leave the tens.

12 − 2 = ☐   18 − 8 = ☐   21 − 1 = ☐

25 − 5 = ☐   33 − 3 = ☐   39 − 9 = ☐

44 − 4 = ☐   47 − 7 = ☐   52 − 2 = ☐

Parent tip
Encourage your child to partition the 2-digit number and then take away the ones.

3 Each 2-digit number has been partitioned.
Write the missing ones.

53 − ☐ = 50   59 − ☐ = 50   65 − ☐ = 60

67 − ☐ = 60   71 − ☐ = 70   78 − ☐ = 70

82 − ☐ = 80   87 − ☐ = 80   93 − ☐ = 90

4 Some numbers have been partitioned into tens and ones.
Write each whole number that was partitioned.

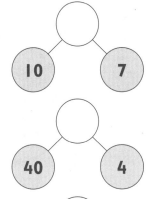 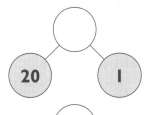 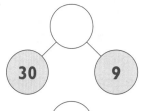

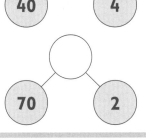 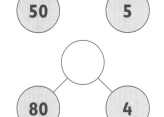 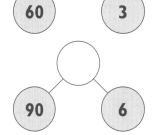

5 Fill in the missing numbers.

☐ − 5 = 10   ☐ − 2 = 20   ☐ − 1 = 30

☐ − 4 = 40   ☐ − 7 = 50   ☐ − 8 = 60

☐ − 3 = 70   ☐ − 6 = 80   ☐ − 9 = 90

6 Fill in the missing numbers.

10 = ☐ − 3   10 = ☐ − 9   20 = ☐ − 1   20 = ☐ − 4

30 = ☐ − 6   30 = ☐ − 9   40 = ☐ − 8   40 = ☐ − 7

50 = ☐ − 2   50 = ☐ − 5   60 = ☐ − 6   60 = ☐ − 2

70 = ☐ − 5   70 = ☐ − 6   80 = ☐ − 8   80 = ☐ − 1

90 = ☐ − 3   90 = ☐ − 7

How much did you do?   Questions 1–6

Circle the star
to show what
you have done.

Some   Most   All

Recombining 2-digit numbers

After partitioning numbers to add or subtract, you recombine the tens and ones to find the whole number.

1 Each picture shows a number as tens and ones.
Write the whole number.

Parent tip
Encourage your child to start at the tens number and count on.

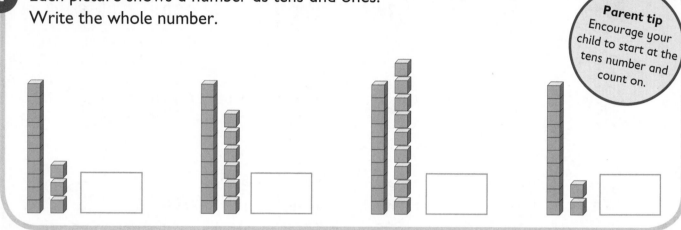

2 Combine the numbers on the 2-digit and 1-digit partitioning cards to make the whole number.

| 2 | 0 | + | 5 | = | |

| 2 | 0 | + | 8 | = | |

| 2 | 0 | + | 2 | = | |

| 2 | 0 | + | 7 | = | |

3 Some two-digit numbers have been partitioned into tens and ones.
Write the whole number in each empty circle.

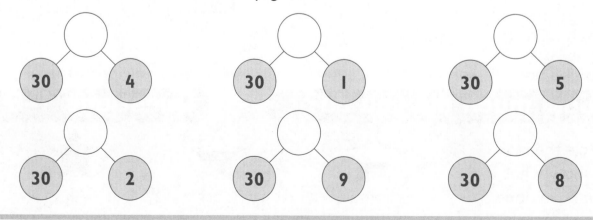

4 Some 2-digit numbers have been partitioned.
Recombine them by adding the tens and ones.

10 and 7 = ☐   10 and 4 = ☐   10 and 1 = ☐

10 and 6 = ☐   10 and 9 = ☐   10 and 5 = ☐

10 and 2 = ☐   10 and 8 = ☐   10 and 3 = ☐

5 Fill in the missing numbers.

50 + ☐ = 54   50 + ☐ = 59   50 + ☐ = 58

60 + ☐ = 61   60 + ☐ = 65   60 + ☐ = 63

40 + ☐ = 48   40 + ☐ = 41   40 + ☐ = 44

6 Add the numbers in words together.
Write the whole number using digits.

seventy + seven = ☐   seventy + one = ☐

eighty + two   = ☐   eighty + four = ☐

ninety + nine = ☐   ninety + five = ☐

Partitioning 3-digit numbers

3-digit numbers can be partitioned into hundreds, tens and ones to help with addition and subtraction.

1 Each picture shows a number that has been partitioned.
Match the picture to the whole number.

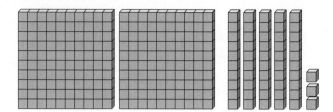

313

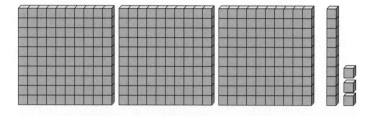

154

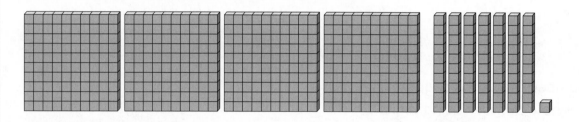

253

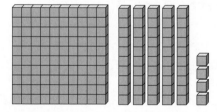

471

Parent tip
Give your child a 3-digit number and ask them to write out the ones, the tens and the hundreds separately.

2 Fill in the missing numbers.

132 $\xrightarrow{-2}$ ☐ $\xrightarrow{-30}$ ☐

247 $\xrightarrow{-7}$ ☐ $\xrightarrow{-40}$ ☐

529 $\xrightarrow{-9}$ ☐ $\xrightarrow{-20}$ ☐

816 $\xrightarrow{-6}$ ☐ $\xrightarrow{-10}$ ☐

3 Partition these numbers into hundreds, tens and ones.

249 = [ ] [ ] [ ] + [ ] [ ] + [ ]

612 = [ ] [ ] [ ] + [ ] [ ] + [ ]

999 = [ ] [ ] [ ] + [ ] [ ] + [ ]

815 = [ ] [ ] [ ] + [ ] [ ] + [ ]

4 Partition these numbers into hundreds, tens and ones. Complete the table.

	Hundreds	Tens	Ones
145	100		
224		20	
523			3
614			
439			
791			

5 Fill in the missing numbers.

719 —−9→ [ ] —−10→ [ ]

863 —−3→ [ ] —−60→ [ ]

Recombining 3-digit numbers

After partitioning numbers to add or subtract, you recombine the hundreds, tens and ones to find the whole number.

1 Combine the numbers on the 3-digit, 2-digit and 1-digit partitioning cards to make the whole number.

| 1 0 0 | + | 4 0 | + | 4 | = | |

| 1 0 0 | + | 6 0 | + | 2 | = | |

| 1 0 0 | + | 9 0 | + | 9 | = | |

| 1 0 0 | + | 7 0 | + | 3 | = | |

2 Some 3-digit numbers have been partitioned.
Recombine them by adding the hundreds, tens and ones.

200, 10 and 7 = ☐   200, 20 and 8 = ☐   200, 50 and 2 = ☐

200, 30 and 1 = ☐   200, 90 and 3 = ☐   200, 40 and 5 = ☐

3 Some numbers have been partitioned into hundreds, tens and ones.
Write each whole number that was partitioned.

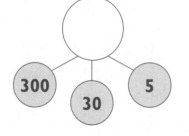
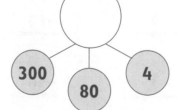
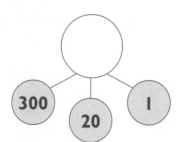

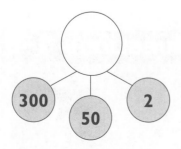
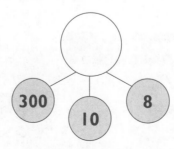
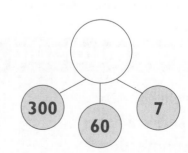

4 Choose one number from each row.
Add your numbers together to make a 3-digit number.
Make five different 3-digit numbers.

| 100 | 200 | 300 | 400 | 500 | 600 | 700 | 800 | 900 |

| 10 | 20 | 30 | 40 | 50 | 60 | 70 | 80 | 90 |

| 1 | 2 | 3 | 4 | 5 | 6 | 7 | 8 | 9 |

[ ] [ ] [ ] [ ] [ ]

5 Fill in the missing numbers.

500 + [ ] + 3 = 543

500 + 80 + 1 = [ ]

[ ] + 30 + 6 = 636

[ ] + 50 + 6 = 556

600 + [ ] + 1 = 671

600 + 10 + 9 = [ ]

6 Add the three numbers in words together.
Write the answer using digits.

seven hundred + twenty + six = [ ]

seven hundred + sixty + seven = [ ]

eight hundred + forty + one = [ ]

two hundred + thirty + nine = [ ]

one hundred + ten + one = [ ]

eight hundred + three = [ ]

nine hundred + ninety + two = [ ]

nine hundred + fifty + four = [ ]

five hundred + eighty + eight = [ ]

six hundred + sixty + zero = [ ]

How much did you do?   **Questions 1–6**

Circle the star
to show what
you have done.

 Some

 Most

 All

Number bonds for 50

Your number bonds for **10** and **5** should help with this topic!

1 Match each key to a keyhole to make 50.

 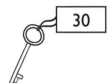 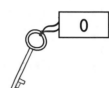 

2 Start at 50 and jump back along the number line. Complete the number sentence.

| 0 | 10 | 20 | 30 | 40 | 50 |

$50 - 30 =$ ▢

| 0 | 10 | 20 | 30 | 40 | 50 |

$50 - 10 =$ ▢

| 0 | 10 | 20 | 30 | 40 | 50 |

$50 - 40 =$ ▢

3 Complete the number sentence for each array.

 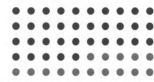

$45 +$ ▢ $= 50$ ▢ $+ 15 = 50$ $35 +$ ▢ $= 50$

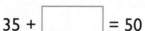

$25 +$ ▢ $= 50$ $5 +$ ▢ $= 50$

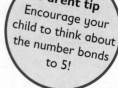

Parent tip
Encourage your child to think about the number bonds to 5!

4 You have 50p to spend on each item.
How much change will you get for each item?
Write and solve a subtraction number sentence to show the answer.

_____

_____

_____

5 There are 50 beads on each abacus. Some have been moved to one side.
Complete the matching number sentences.

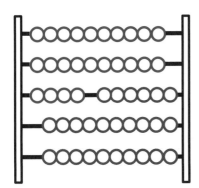

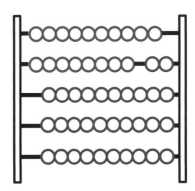

24 + ☐ = 50   18 + ☐ = 50

6 Fill in the missing numbers.

50 – 13 = ☐   50 – 26 = ☐   50 – 35 = ☐

50 – ☐ = 8   50 – ☐ = 19   50 – ☐ = 32

How much did you do?   Questions 1-6

Circle the star
to show what
you have done.

Some

Most

All

Number bonds for 100

Parent tip
Encourage your child to think about the number bonds for 10!

1 Each bead represents 10.
Complete the number sentences.

100 − 20 = ☐

100 − 90 = ☐

100 − 50 = ☐

100 − 60 = ☐

2 Match the shoes so that each pair makes 100.

 10
 30
 20
 50
 100

 70
 50
 80
 0
 90

3 Fill in the missing numbers.

100 − 5 = ☐

100 − 25 = ☐

100 − 35 = ☐

100 − ☐ = 45

100 − ☐ = 85

4 Match the numbers so that each pair adds up to 100.

(45)　(25)　(55)　(15)　(75)

(35)　(85)　(5)　(65)　(95)

5 See how quickly you can make your way around the race track by completing the calculations.

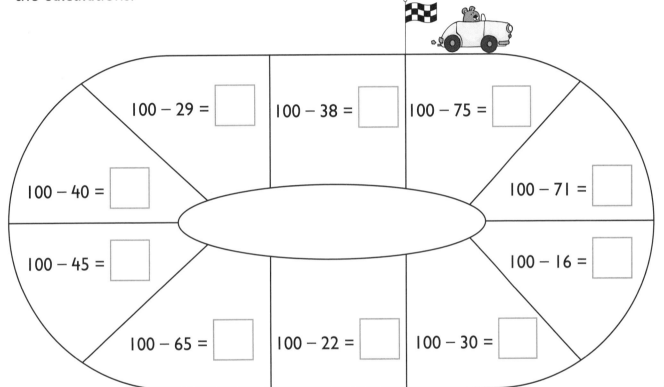

$100 - 29 =$ ☐

$100 - 38 =$ ☐

$100 - 75 =$ ☐

$100 - 40 =$ ☐

$100 - 71 =$ ☐

$100 - 45 =$ ☐

$100 - 16 =$ ☐

$100 - 65 =$ ☐

$100 - 22 =$ ☐

$100 - 30 =$ ☐

6 Fill in the missing numbers.

$100 =$ ☐ $+ 73$　　$100 = 12 +$ ☐　　$100 =$ ☐ $+ 36$

$100 = 25 +$ ☐　　$100 =$ ☐ $+ 84$　　$100 = 57 +$ ☐

Doubles and halves

When a number is added to itself, it is doubled. Halving is the inverse of doubling – it splits a number into two equal halves.

1 Add the numbers on each pair of dice to find the double.

 + = ☐   + = ☐

+ = ☐   + = ☐

+ = ☐   + = ☐

2 Halve each of these numbers.
Write a subtraction number sentence underneath.

Half of 4 = | 2 | Half of 6 = ☐   Half of 10 = ☐

4 – | 2 | = | 2 | 6 – ☐ = ☐   10 – ☐ = ☐

Half of 8 = ☐   Half of 2 = ☐   Half of 12 = ☐

8 – ☐ = ☐   2 – ☐ = ☐   12 – ☐ = ☐

3 Look at the sums.
Colour each part of the
football that shows a double.

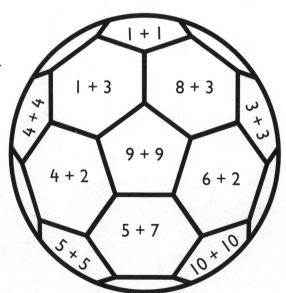

1 + 1

1 + 3   8 + 3

4 + 4

3 + 3

9 + 9

4 + 2   6 + 2

5 + 7

5 + 5   10 + 10

Parent tip
Play 'I say, you say' with your child. This time, ask them to double the number you say.

4 Draw a line from each label to the
parcel that shows the correct answer.

5 Count the dots on the butterfly's wing.
Draw the same number of dots on the other wing. Fill in the missing numbers.

Double ☐ = ☐

Double ☐ = ☐

Double ☐ = ☐

Double ☐ = ☐

Double ☐ = ☐

Double ☐ = ☐

6 Draw a line to match each calculation to the correct answer.

(10 − 5) (6 + 6) (12 − 6) (8 + 8) (20 − 10)

(10) (16) (12) (6) (5)

Adding ones

When adding ones to a **2-digit number**, sometimes the ones will cross the next ten, e.g. **19 + 2 = 21**

1 Add the one to the 2-digit number.

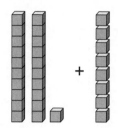

☐ + ☐ = ☐

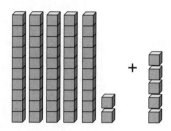

☐ + ☐ = ☐

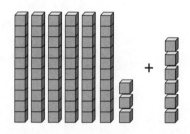

☐ + ☐ = ☐

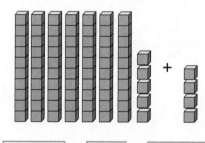

☐ + ☐ = ☐

2 Complete the number pyramids by adding the two blue numbers together.

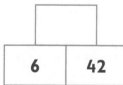

5	22
9	39
6	42

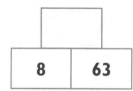

7	50
8	63
4	79

3 Fill in the missing numbers.

29 + 3 = ☐   56 + 8 = ☐   36 + 7 = ☐

66 + 5 = ☐   48 + 4 = ☐   79 + 9 = ☐

4 Choose a number from the 2-digit wheel.
Add a number from the 1-digit wheel.
Write the calculation and answer.

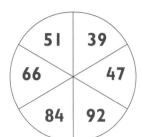
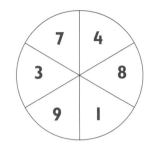

☐ + ☐ = ☐

☐ + ☐ = ☐

☐ + ☐ = ☐

☐ + ☐ = ☐

☐ + ☐ = ☐

☐ + ☐ = ☐

5 The top bar shows a whole number.
The two bars under it make the same total.
Write the missing numbers.

47	
39	

62	
	56

84	
75	

95	
	88

6 Fill in the missing numbers.

37 = 28 + ☐   39 = 31 + ☐   51 = 45 + ☐

57 = 68 + ☐   64 = 58 + ☐   75 = 67 + ☐

Subtracting ones

1 Start at the total and jump back along the number line to subtract.

| 21 | 22 | 23 | 24 | 25 | 26 | 27 | 28 | 29 | 30 |

30 – 9 = ☐

| 21 | 22 | 23 | 24 | 25 | 26 | 27 | 28 | 29 | 30 |

26 – 4 = ☐

| 21 | 22 | 23 | 24 | 25 | 26 | 27 | 28 | 29 | 30 |

29 – 7 = ☐

| 21 | 22 | 23 | 24 | 25 | 26 | 27 | 28 | 29 | 30 |

25 – 4 = ☐

2 Complete the number pyramids by subtracting the bottom number from the top number. Write the answer in the empty box.

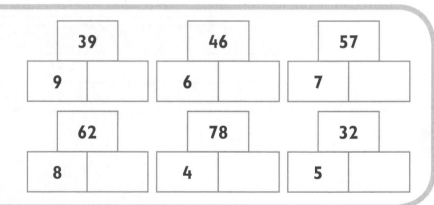

| 39 | | 46 | | 57 | |
| 9 | | 6 | | 7 | |

| 62 | | 78 | | 32 | |
| 8 | | 4 | | 5 | |

3 Complete the calculations.

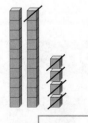   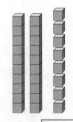   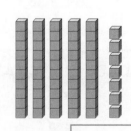   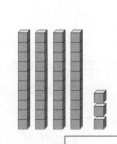

24 – 5 = ☐   28 – 9 = ☐   57 – 8 = ☐   43 – 7 = ☐

4 Match the racing car to the driver's helmet to complete the subtractions.

 25 − 4   93 − 7   77 − 8   83 − 5   41 − 3

38   21   78   86   69

5 Count back from the larger number to the smaller number.
Complete the subtractions and balance the scales.

55 − ☐ = 46   51 − ☐ = 47   67 − ☐ = 59

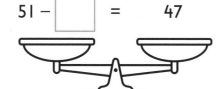 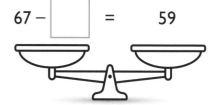

63 − ☐ = 56   75 − ☐ = 66   78 − ☐ = 70

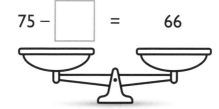 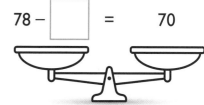

6 Fill in the missing numbers.

76 − 3 = ☐   36 = 42 − ☐

33 − 8 = ☐   68 = 75 − ☐

51 − 4 = ☐   88 = 94 − ☐

> **Parent tip**
> Partition the ones to reach the ten, e.g.
> 33 − 8 = 33 − 3 − 5
> = 30 − 5

How much did you do?   ## Questions 1–6

Circle the star to show what you have done.

 Some   Most   All

Adding tens

When you add a tens number to a 2-digit number, the ones remain the same!

1 Here is part of a 100 square. Add 10 to each blue number by colouring in the number beneath it. Complete the number sentences.

1	2	3	4	5	6	7	8	9	10
11	12	13	**14**	15	16	17	18	**19**	20
21	22	23	24	25	**26**	27	28	**29**	30
31	32	33	34	35	36	37	38	39	40

14 + 10 = ☐   19 + 10 = ☐   26 + 10 = ☐   29 + 10 = ☐

2 Add 10 by drawing another bead on each tens spike. Complete the number sentences.

  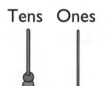

12 + 10 = ☐   23 + 10 = ☐   46 + 10 = ☐   52 + 10 = ☐

3 Add the tens. Complete the number sentences.

Parent tip
Discuss with your child which representation they find most helpful. Encourage them to use it when solving future problems.

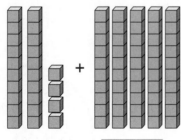

24 + 50 = ☐

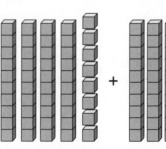

48 + 30 = ☐

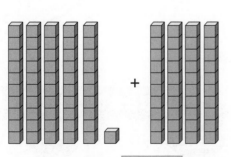

51 + 40 = ☐

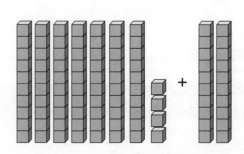

74 + 20 = ☐

4 Start with the black number on the left each time.
Work along the row, adding the different tens.

	+ 10	+ 20	+ 30	+ 40	+ 50	+ 60	+ 70	+ 80
13	23	33	43					
15								
18								

5 Fill in the missing numbers.

36 + 30 = ☐   57 + 40 = ☐   51 + 20 = ☐

84 = 20 + ☐   62 = 40 + ☐   97 = 70 + ☐

6 Complete the calculations.
You can use any method.

41 + 40

68 + 30

Subtracting tens

When subtracting a tens number from a 2-digit number, the ones will remain the same!

1 Here is part of a 100 square.
Subtract 10 from each blue number by colouring the number above it.
Complete the number sentence.

1	2	3	4	5	6	7	8	9	10
11	12	13	14	15	16	17	18	19	20
21	22	23	24	25	26	27	**28**	29	30
31	32	33	34	35	**36**	37	38	39	**40**

11 − 10 = ☐   28 − 10 = ☐   36 − 10 = ☐   40 − 10 = ☐

2 Jump back on the number line to solve the subtractions.

5 6 7 8 9 10 11 12 13 14 15 16 17 18 19 20 21 22 23 24 25

20 − 10 = ☐

10 11 12 13 14 15 16 17 18 19 20 21 22 23 24 25 26 27 28 29 30

25 − 10 = ☐

15 16 17 18 19 20 21 22 23 24 25 26 27 28 29 30

29 − 10 = ☐

20 21 22 23 24 25 26 27 28 29 30 31 32 33 34 35

34 − 10 = ☐

3 Subtract the tens by crossing out the matching number of beads on each tens spike.
Complete the number sentences.

Tens Ones   Tens Ones   Tens Ones   Tens Ones

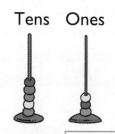
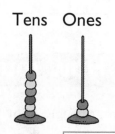

24 − 20 = ☐   31 − 20 = ☐   53 − 30 = ☐   62 − 40 = ☐

4 Match each tennis racket to a tennis ball to subtract the tens.

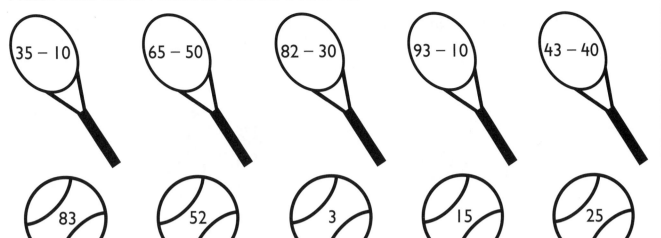

35 – 10   65 – 50   82 – 30   93 – 10   43 – 40

83   52   3   15   25

5 Choose a number from the 2-digit target.
Subtract a number from the tens target.
Write the calculation and answer.

☐ – ☐ = ☐

☐ – ☐ = ☐

☐ – ☐ = ☐

☐ – ☐ = ☐

☐ – ☐ = ☐

☐ – ☐ = ☐

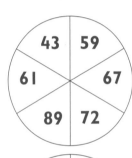

43	59
61	67
89	72

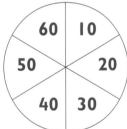

60	10
50	20
40	30

6 Fill in the missing numbers.

76 – 30 = ☐   93 – 40 = ☐   81 – 70 = ☐

84 = 94 – ☐   33 = 63 – ☐   55 = 95 – ☐

How much did you do?   **Questions 1–6**

Circle the star to show what you have done.

 Some   Most   All

Adding two 2-digit numbers

Now you are going to add two 2-digit numbers!

1 Add the two amounts. Complete the number sentence.

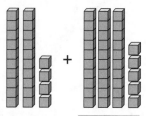

24 + 35 = ☐

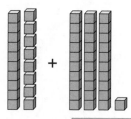

18 + 31 = ☐

Parent tip
See if your child can spot any number bonds!

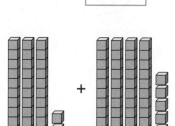

32 + 45 = ☐

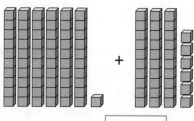

61 + 36 = ☐

2 Draw beads on the abacus spikes to add the second number. Write the total.

Tens Ones   Tens Ones   Tens Ones   Tens Ones

14 + 45 = ☐

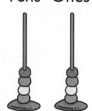

44 + 12 = ☐

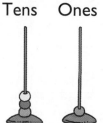

31 + 22 = ☐

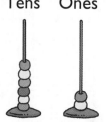

62 + 34 = ☐

3 Complete each calculation.

```
    2  4            3  4            1  2
 +  1  3         +  4  2         +  2  7
 _____        _____        _____

 _____        _____        _____


    5  3            7  1            6  3
 +  3  6         +  1  8         +  3  5
 _____        _____        _____

 _____        _____        _____
```

4 Add the bottom numbers together.
Write the answer in the empty box.

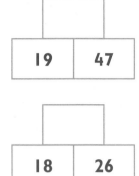

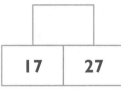

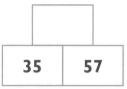

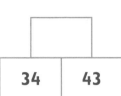

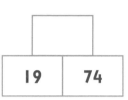

5 Fill in the missing numbers.

$47 + 33 = \boxed{}$

$55 + 45 = \boxed{}$

$21 + 39 = \boxed{}$

$72 = 27 + \boxed{}$

$89 = 46 + \boxed{}$

$51 = 34 + \boxed{}$

6 Complete each calculation.

```
    4  8          6  2          1  4
+   3  2      +   1  9      +   5  7
_____    _____    _____


_____    _____    _____


    3  8          7  2          2  9
+   3  5      +   1  9      +   5  5
_____    _____    _____


_____    _____    _____
```

How much did you do?

Questions 1-6

Circle the star
to show what
you have done.

 Some

 Most

 All

Subtracting two 2-digit numbers

1 Jump back on the number line to solve the subtractions.

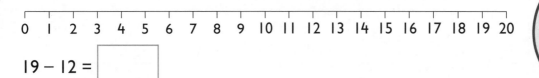

0 1 2 3 4 5 6 7 8 9 10 11 12 13 14 15 16 17 18 19 20

19 − 12 = ☐

Parent tip
Ask your child to check their answer by making the calculation into an addition, e.g. 19 − 12 = 7, so 7 + 12 = 19

10 11 12 13 14 15 16 17 18 19 20 21 22 23 24 25 26 27 28 29 30

29 − 15 = ☐

20 21 22 23 24 25 26 27 28 29 30 31 32 33 34 35 36 37 38 39 40 41 42 43 44 45 46 47 48 49 50 51 52 53 54 55

53 − 32 = ☐

2 Complete the subtractions and balance the scales.

73 − ☐ = 20   58 − ☐ = 37   67 − ☐ = 59

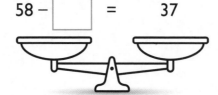
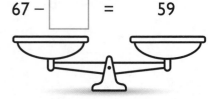

64 − ☐ = 46   25 − ☐ = 16   39 − ☐ = 10

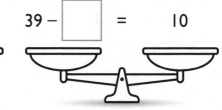

3 Draw a line from each subtraction to the correct answer.

(34 − 13)   (56 − 36)   (89 − 46)   (18 − 15)

(43)   (3)   (21)   (20)

4 The top bar shows a total. The two bars under it make that total. Write the missing numbers.

36	
27	

24	
	11

68	
38	

19	
	12

5 Write the missing numbers.

$42 - 32 = \boxed{}$ $59 - 41 = \boxed{}$ $88 - 75 = \boxed{}$

$36 = 57 - \boxed{}$ $46 = 79 - \boxed{}$ $33 = 99 - \boxed{}$

6 Complete each calculation.

```
    5  7            6  2            4  8
 -  2  3         -  3  1         -  1  2
 _____       _____       _____

 _____       _____       _____


    3  8            7  8            5  9
 -  3  5         -  2  4         -  2  5
 _____       _____       _____

 _____       _____       _____
```

More doubles and halves

Doubling is adding two numbers that are the same. Halving is partitioning a quantity to give two numbers that are the same.

1 Follow the footpath by doubling or halving the numbers.
You could even race a friend!

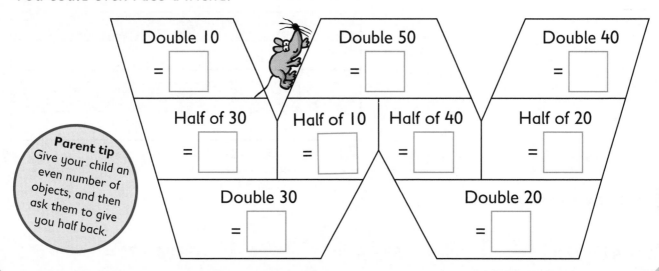

Double 10 = ☐   Double 50 = ☐   Double 40 = ☐

Half of 30 = ☐   Half of 10 = ☐   Half of 40 = ☐   Half of 20 = ☐

Double 30 = ☐   Double 20 = ☐

Parent tip
Give your child an even number of objects, and then ask them to give you half back.

2 Partition these numbers into tens and ones.
Double the tens and ones. Then, recombine them!

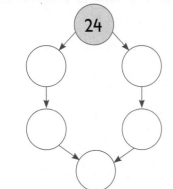

24

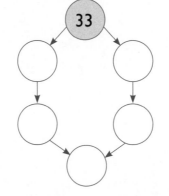

33

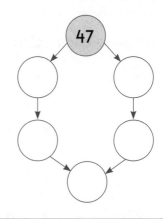

47

3 Double or halve each of these numbers. Write the matching calculation underneath.

Double 24 = ☐   Double 35 = ☐   Double 42 = ☐

24 + ☐ = ☐   35 + ☐ = ☐   42 + ☐ = ☐

Half of 28 = ☐   Half of 36 = ☐   Half of 42 = ☐

28 − ☐ = ☐   36 − ☐ = ☐   42 − ☐ = ☐

Start at 5.
Follow the instructions
to reach the final answer.

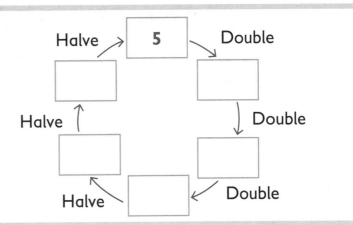

Halve → [5] Double
[ ]
Halve ↑ Double ↓
[ ]
Halve ← [ ] ← Double

Complete the sentences.

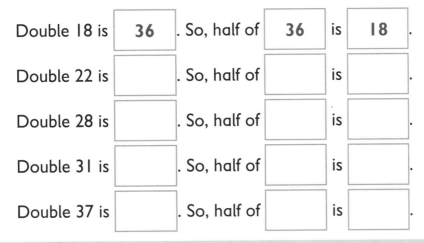

Double 18 is [36]. So, half of [36] is [18].

Double 22 is [ ]. So, half of [ ] is [ ].

Double 28 is [ ]. So, half of [ ] is [ ].

Double 31 is [ ]. So, half of [ ] is [ ].

Double 37 is [ ]. So, half of [ ] is [ ].

The first machine doubles numbers.
The second machine halves numbers.
Write the numbers that come out of the machines.

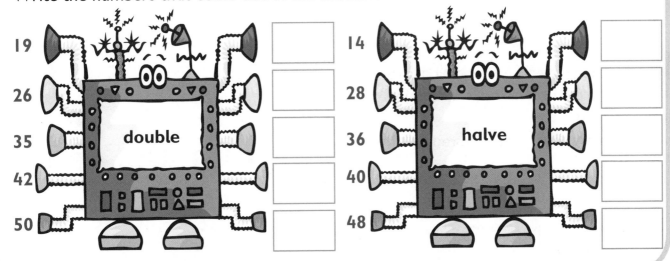

19 | double | [ ]
26 | | [ ]
35 | | [ ]
42 | | [ ]
50 | | [ ]

14 | halve | [ ]
28 | | [ ]
36 | | [ ]
40 | | [ ]
48 | | [ ]

How much did you do?   ## Questions 1–6

Circle the star
to show what
you have done.

 Some   Most   All

49

More one-step problems

Think carefully about what you are being asked. Will you need to add or subtract to solve the problem?

1 Amina collects 18 daisies to make a chain.
Her brother gives her 3 more.

How many daisies does Amina now have?

[ ] daisies

Parent tip
Encourage your child to draw the problem or use objects to 'act' it out.

2 Lydia has 95 marbles.
She loses 25 marbles when she is playing outside.

How many marbles does Lydia have left?

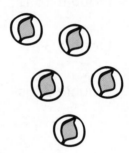

[ ] marbles

3 A teacher collects 28 tennis balls for a PE lesson.
There are 22 tennis balls already in the sports hall.

How many balls does the teacher have altogether?

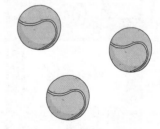

[ ] balls

4 Amy scores a total of 69 points in archery.
Anisa scores 309 points.

How many more points did Anisa score than Amy?

| | points

5 Abdul has 44 stamps in his collection.
His little sister has half that amount.

How many stamps does Abdul's sister have?

| | stamps

6 Jack is driving his truck.
He stops for a break after 38 miles, which is half way there,
and then drives to his destination.

How far did Jack travel altogether?

| | miles

How much did you do?   Questions 1-6

Circle the star
to show what
you have done.

 Some

 Most

 All

51

Adding three 1-digit numbers

1 Add the three quantities.
Look for a number bond for 10 to help you.

○○○○ + ○○○○○○○○○ + ○○○○○○ = ☐

○○○ + ○○○○○ + ○○○○○○○○ = ☐

○○○○○○○○○○○ + ○○○○○ + ○ = ☐

○○○○○○○ + ○○○○○○○○○ + ○○○○○○ = ☐

Parent tip
Encourage your child to look for a number bond or a double that they already know. They can then count on for the third number.

2 Add the three groups of ones.
Write the answer.

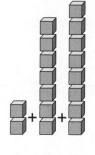 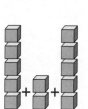 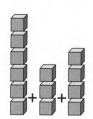 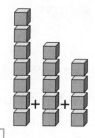

2 + 7 + 8 = ☐   5 + 2 + 5 = ☐   6 + 3 + 4 = ☐   7 + 5 + 4 = ☐

3 Choose a number from each target and add them together.
Write the calculation and answer.

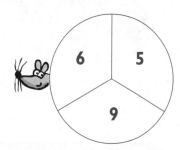   

☐ + ☐ + ☐ = ☐   ☐ + ☐ + ☐ = ☐

☐ + ☐ + ☐ = ☐   ☐ + ☐ + ☐ = ☐

4 Add the numbers on the petals together.
Write the answer in the centre of the flower.

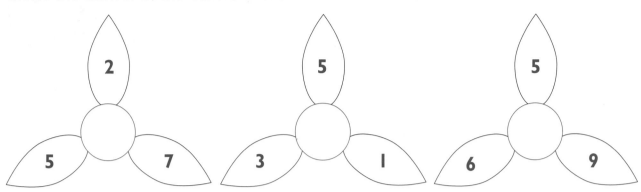

5 Complete the number pyramids.
Add numbers that are next to each other.
Write the answers in the row above.

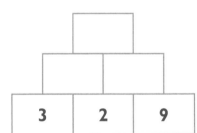 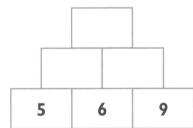 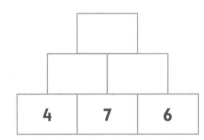

6 Fill in the missing numbers.

16 = 5 + 6 + ☐   13 = 4 + 3 + ☐   21 = 7 + 9 + ☐

18 = 2 + 9 + ☐   23 = 9 + 8 + ☐   26 = 9 + 8 + ☐

19 = 7 + 4 + ☐   25 = 9 + 7 + ☐   15 = 4 + 7 + ☐

Two-step problems

Think carefully about what you are being asked. Will you need to add or subtract to solve the problem?

1 In a football team, there are 9 players who are right footed, 7 players who are left footed and 8 players who can use both feet.

How many players are in the team in total?

| | players

2 89 books are borrowed from a library.
24 of the books are returned after a week.
33 of the books are returned a week after that.

How many books have **not** been returned?

| | books

3 On Monday, 60 people visited a cinema.
35 people went to the cinema in the morning.
12 people went to the cinema in the afternoon.

Parent tip
Encourage your child to write a number sentence for the problem.

How many people went to the cinema in the evening?

| | people

4 A carpenter needs 78 planks of wood to make the ground floor of a building, 25 for the second floor and 23 for the third floor.

How many planks does the carpenter need altogether?

[ ] planks of wood

5 Aisha has £78.
She pays £34 for her car to be fixed.
She then has to pay £13 for a new part for her washing machine.

How much money does she have left?

£ [ ]

6 Marin grows apples in his orchard.
He picks 59 apples off the trees.
He sells 38 apples to one shop and 10 to another shop.

How many of the apples does Marin have left?

[ ] apples

How much did you do?   Questions 1–6

Circle the star
to show what
you have done.   Some   Most   All

Commutativity

Some calculations can be carried out in any order and in many ways. However, others cannot.

1 Find two more ways that each calculation can be carried out.
The first one has been done for you.

$5 + 2 + 1 =$ | 2 | + | 1 | + | 5 | = | 1 | + | 2 | + | 5 |

$3 + 4 + 3 =$ ☐ + ☐ + ☐ = ☐ + ☐ + ☐

$7 + 5 + 8 =$ ☐ + ☐ + ☐ = ☐ + ☐ + ☐

$6 + 2 + 9 =$ ☐ + ☐ + ☐ = ☐ + ☐ + ☐

2 Solve each calculation.
Then find another way to complete it.
The first one has been done for you.

$7 + 6 =$ | 13 | | 6 | $+ 7 =$ | 13 |

$9 + 8 =$ ☐   ☐ $+ 9 =$ ☐

$5 + 3 =$ ☐   ☐ $+ 5 =$ ☐

$8 + 4 =$ ☐   ☐ $+ 8 =$ ☐

Parent tip
Write the numbers from a calculation on three separate cards. Encourage your child to move them into different positions to make new number sentences!

3 Write a subtraction that is the reverse of each addition.
The first one has been done for you.

$7 + 6 = 13$ $13 -$ | 6 | $= 7$

$4 + 8 = 12$ $12 -$ ☐ $= 4$

$5 + 9 = 14$ $14 -$ ☐ $= 5$

4 Use the numbers from each addition to write two subtractions.
The first one has been done for you.

$15 + 7 = 22$ $\boxed{22} - 7 = \boxed{15}$ $\boxed{22} - 15 = \boxed{7}$

$18 + 6 = 24$ $\boxed{} - 6 = \boxed{}$ $\boxed{} - 18 = \boxed{}$

$24 + 9 = 33$ $\boxed{} - 9 = \boxed{}$ $\boxed{} - 24 = \boxed{}$

5 Use each set of three numbers to write two addition and two subtraction calculations.

15   25   40   27   22   49

$\boxed{} + \boxed{} = \boxed{}$ $\boxed{} + \boxed{} = \boxed{}$

$\boxed{} + \boxed{} = \boxed{}$ $\boxed{} + \boxed{} = \boxed{}$

$\boxed{} - \boxed{} = \boxed{}$ $\boxed{} - \boxed{} = \boxed{}$

$\boxed{} - \boxed{} = \boxed{}$ $\boxed{} - \boxed{} = \boxed{}$

6 Complete each calculation.
Then use the same numbers to write another addition and two subtractions.

$33 + 53 = \boxed{}$ $47 + 39 = \boxed{}$

$\boxed{} + \boxed{} = \boxed{}$ $\boxed{} + \boxed{} = \boxed{}$

$\boxed{} - \boxed{} = \boxed{}$ $\boxed{} - \boxed{} = \boxed{}$

$\boxed{} - \boxed{} = \boxed{}$ $\boxed{} - \boxed{} = \boxed{}$

How much did you do?   Questions 1–6

Circle the star to show what you have done.

 Some   Most   All

Addition and subtraction within 100

Use all your addition facts, doubles and number bonds to help you with these questions.

1 Complete the calculations.

3 + 3 = 6, so 30 + 30 = ☐   4 + 4 = 8, so 40 + 40 = ☐

2 + 2 = 4, so 20 + 20 = ☐

2 Complete the calculations.

8 − 3 = 5, so 80 − 30 = ☐   6 − 3 = 3, so 60 − 30 = ☐

9 − 2 = 7, so 90 − 20 = ☐   4 − 1 = 3, so 40 − 10 = ☐

7 − 6 = 1, so 70 − 60 = ☐   10 − 4 = 6, so 100 − 40 = ☐

3 Complete the calculations.
Try and use your number bonds for 10 to help you.

23 + 47 = ☐   36 + 54 = ☐   11 + 89 = ☐

45 + 35 = ☐   32 + 58 = ☐   77 + 13 = ☐

54 + 16 = ☐   29 + 21 = ☐   48 + 32 = ☐

65 + 25 = ☐   30 + 20 = ☐

Parent tip
Try partitioning the 2-digit numbers. Add the ones and the tens and then recombine the two numbers.

58

4 Complete the calculations.
First add 10, and then subtract 1!

32 + 9 = ☐   54 + 9 = ☐   87 + 9 = ☐

48 + 9 = ☐   65 + 9 = ☐   77 + 9 = ☐

5 Complete the calculations.
First subtract 10, and then add 1!

30 − 9 = ☐   50 − 9 = ☐   80 − 9 = ☐

40 − 9 = ☐   60 − 9 = ☐   70 − 9 = ☐

32 − 9 = ☐   54 − 9 = ☐   87 − 9 = ☐

48 − 9 = ☐   65 − 9 = ☐   77 − 9 = ☐

6 Complete the calculations.
Try using doubles to help you!

20 + 25 = ☐   30 + 34 = ☐   20 + 29 = ☐

40 + 42 = ☐   30 + 38 = ☐   40 + 48 = ☐

Answers

One more

Page 4

1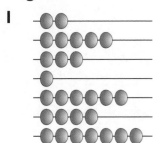

2 One more spot drawn on each ladybird;
7, 10, 9, 8

3 20, 16, 14

Page 5

4 28 + 1 = 29, 32 + 1 = 33, 39 + 1 = 40,
40 + 1 = 41, 47 + 1 = 48

5 49, 64, 58, 69, 60, 73

6 70, 75, 82, 87, 98

One less

Page 6

1 3, 5, 0, 4

2 2, 8, 6, 9

3 18, 14, 16, 12

Page 7

4 20 − 1 = 19, 35 − 1 = 34, 38 − 1 = 37,
44 − 1 = 43, 47 − 1 = 46

5 49, 63, 56, 72, 60, 77

6 60, 21, 42, 15, 74

Number bonds for 5 and 10

Page 8

1 4 + 1 = 5, 2 + 3 = 5, 1 + 4 = 5, 0 + 5 = 5

2 5 − 3 = 2, 5 − 4 = 1, 5 − 2 = 3, 5 − 1 = 4

3 4, 1, 5, 2, 4, 5

Page 9

4 7 + 3 = 10 and 3 + 7 = 10, 8 + 2 = 10 and
2 + 8 = 10, 4 + 6 = 10 and 6 + 4 = 10

5 10 − 2 = 8, 10 − 8 = 2, 10 − 9 = 1, 10 − 7 = 3

6 9, 7, 6, 9, 10, 10

Addition and subtraction within 10

Page 10

1 7, 5, 3, 9, 9, 7

2 5, 9, 1

3 9, 7, 3, 9, 7

Page 11

4 6, 2, 8, 3, 0, 10

5 Going in a clockwise direction: 8, 9, 7, 4,
8, 9, 9, 8, 8, 7

6 10 − 5 and 3 + 2 = 5 (black),
4 − 1 = 3 (white), 8 − 1, 1 + 6 and
4 + 3 = 7 (red), 10 − 2 = 8 (blue), 3 + 1
and 2 + 2 = 4 (green), 5 + 4 = 9 (orange)

Number bonds for 20

Page 12

1 10, 19, 15, 5

2 0 + 20, 2 + 18, 17 + 3, 16 + 4, 19 + 1

3 20 + 0, 8 + 12, 13 + 7, 11 + 9, 14 + 6

Page 13

4 19, 5, 16, 13, 6, 12

5 13, 3, 9, 8

6 8, 9, 17, 16, 14, 2

Addition and subtraction within 20

Page 14

1 5 + 13 = 18, 8 + 8 = 16, 20 + 0 = 20,
13 + 4 = 17, 12 + 7 = 19, 14 + 1 = 15

2 11, 3, 17, 11, 5, 13

3 14 − 6 = 8, 12 − 9 = 3, 17 − 8 = 9

Page 15

4 10p, 15p, 12p, 11p

5 6, 7, 8, 3, 8, 2

6 9 + 7 = 16, 5 + 7 = 12, 9 + 9 = 18, 3 + 8 = 11

One-step problems

Page 16

1 16 football cards

2 17 marbles

3 15 sweets

Page 17

4 6 toy horses

5 20 strawberries

6 7p

Counting on

Page 18

1. 6, 8, 10, 12, 14, 16, 18, 20
2. 5, 10, 15, 20, 25, 30, 35, 40, 45, 50
3. 3, 6, 9, 12, 15, 18, 21, 24, 27, 30

Page 19

4. 10, 20, 30, 40, 50, 60, 70, 80, 90, 100
5. 10 jumps of 2, 6 jumps of 5
6. 10 groups of 3, 3 groups of 10

Counting back

Page 20

1. 22, 20, 18, 16, 14, 12, 10, 8, 6, 4, 2, 0
2. Rings around 30, 27, 24, 21, 18, 15, 12, 9, 6 and 3
3. 18 jumps of 2, 12 jumps of 3

Page 21

4. 55, 40, 30, 10, 5
   85, 55, 40
5. Circles around the numbers: 100, 90, 80, 70, 60, 50, 40, 30, 20 and 10
   Squares around the numbers: 100, 95, 90, 85, 80, 75, 70, 65, 60, 55, 50, 45, 40, 35, 30, 25, 20, 15, 10 and 5

6.
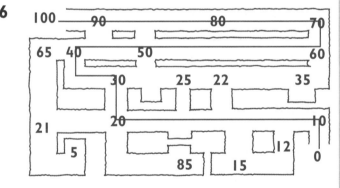

Partitioning 2-digit numbers

Page 22

1. 10 and 4, 20 and 3, 30 and 5, 40 and 2, 50 and 9, 60 and 7, 70 and 1, 80 and 6, 90 and 8
2. 10, 10, 20, 20, 30, 30, 40, 40, 50
3. 3, 9, 5, 7, 1, 8, 2, 7, 3

Page 23

4. 17, 21, 39, 44, 55, 63, 72, 84, 96
5. 15, 22, 31, 44, 57, 68, 73, 86, 99
6. 13, 19, 21, 24, 36, 39, 48, 47, 52, 55, 66, 62, 75, 76, 88, 81, 93, 97

Recombining 2-digit numbers

Page 24

1. 13, 16, 19, 12
2. 25, 28, 22, 27
3. 34, 31, 35, 32, 39, 38

Page 25

4. 17, 14, 11, 16, 19, 15, 12, 18, 13
5. 4, 9, 8, 1, 5, 3, 8, 1, 4
6. 77, 71, 82, 84, 99, 95

Partitioning 3-digit numbers

Page 26

1.
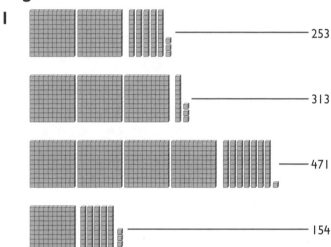

2. 130 and 100, 240 and 200, 520 and 500, 810 and 800

Page 27

3. 200 + 40 + 9, 600 + 10 + 2, 900 + 90 + 9, 800 + 10 + 5

4.

	Hundreds	Tens	Ones
145	100	40	5
224	200	20	4
523	500	20	3
614	600	10	4
439	400	30	9
791	700	90	1

5. 710 and 700, 860 and 800

Recombining 3-digit numbers

Page 28

1. 144, 162, 199, 173
2. 217, 228, 252, 231, 293, 245
3. 335, 384, 321, 352, 318, 367

Page 29

4 Accept any answers from 111 to 999

5 40, 500, 581, 70, 600, 619

6 726, 803, 767, 992, 841, 954, 239, 588, 111, 660

Number bonds for 50
Page 30

1 10 + 40, 50 + 0, 20 + 30

2 20, 40, 10

3 5, 35, 15, 25, 45

Page 31

4 $50 - 25 = 25p$, $50 - 45 = 5p$, $50 - 15 = 35p$

5 26, 32

6 37, 24, 15, 42, 31, 18

Number bonds for 100
Page 32

1 80, 10, 50, 40

2 10 + 90, 30 + 70, 20 + 80, 50 + 50, 100 + 0

3 95, 75, 65, 55, 15

Page 33

4 45 + 55, 35 + 65, 75 + 25, 85 + 15, 5 + 95

5 Going in a clockwise direction: 25, 29, 84, 70, 78, 35, 55, 60, 71, 62

6 27, 88, 64, 75, 16, 43

Doubles and halves
Page 34

1 6, 2, 4, 8, 12, 10

2 $3, 6 - 3 = 3$, $5, 10 - 5 = 5$, $4, 8 - 4 = 4$, $1, 2 - 1 = 1$, $6, 12 - 6 = 6$

3 The following areas should be coloured: 1 + 1, 4 + 4, 5 + 5, 10 + 10, 3 + 3, 9 + 9

Page 35

4 $20 - 10 = 10$, $12 - 6 = 6$, $16 - 8 = 8$, $18 - 9 = 9$, $14 - 7 = 7$

5 Double 8 = 16, Double 2 = 4, Double 5 = 10, Double 6 = 12, Double 10 = 20, Double 9 = 18

6 $10 - 5 = 5$, $6 + 6 = 12$, $12 - 6 = 6$, $8 + 8 = 16$, $20 - 10 = 10$

Adding ones
Page 36

1 $21 + 8 = 29$, $52 + 5 = 57$, $63 + 6 = 69$, $75 + 4 = 79$

2 27, 48, 48, 57, 71, 83

3 32, 64, 43, 71, 52, 88

Page 37

4 Accept any correct addition calculations using the numbers provided

5 8, 6, 9, 7

6 9, 8, 6, 9, 6, 8

Subtracting ones
Page 38

1 21, 22, 22, 21

2 30, 40, 50, 54, 74, 27

3 19, 19, 49, 36

Page 39

4 $25 - 4 = 21$, $93 - 7 = 86$, $77 - 8 = 69$, $83 - 5 = 78$, $41 - 3 = 38$

5 9, 4, 8, 7, 9, 8

6 73, 6, 25, 7, 47, 6

Adding tens
Page 40

1 24, 29, 36, 39

2 22, 33, 56, 62

3 74, 78, 91, 94

Page 41

4 53, 63, 73, 83, 93
25, 35, 45, 55, 65, 75, 85, 95
28, 38, 48, 58, 68, 78, 88, 98

5 66, 97, 71, 64, 22, 27

6 81, 98

Subtracting tens
Page 42

1 1, 18, 26, 30

2 10, 15, 19, 24

3 4, 11, 23, 22

Page 43

4 $35 - 10 = 25$, $65 - 50 = 15$, $82 - 30 = 52$, $93 - 10 = 83$, $43 - 40 = 3$

5 Accept any correct subtraction calculations using the numbers provided.

6 46, 53, 11, 10, 30, 40

Adding two 2-digit numbers
Page 44

1 59, 49, 77, 97

2 59, 56, 53, 96

3 37, 76, 39, 89, 89, 98

Page 45

4 66, 44, 92, 44, 77, 93

5 80, 100, 60, 45, 43, 17

6 80, 81, 71, 73, 91, 84

Subtracting two 2-digit numbers

Page 46

1 7, 14, 21

2 53, 21, 8, 18, 9, 29

3 34 − 13 = 21, 56 − 36 = 20, 89 − 46 = 43, 18 − 15 = 3

Page 47

4 9, 13, 30, 7

5 10, 18, 13, 21, 33, 66

6 34, 31, 36, 3, 54, 34

More doubles and halves

Page 48

1 20, 15, 60, 5, 100, 20, 40, 10, 80

2

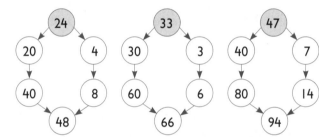

3 48 and 24 + 24 = 48, 70 and 35 + 35 = 70, 84 and 42 + 42 = 84, 14 and 28 − 14 = 14, 18 and 36 − 18 = 18, 21 and 42 − 21 = 21

Page 49

4 10, 20, 40, 20, 10

5 44, 44 and 22, 56, 56 and 28, 62, 62 and 31, 74, 74 and 37

6 Doubling machine: 38, 52, 70, 84, 100
Halving machine: 7, 14, 18, 20, 24

More one-step problems

Page 50

1 21 daisies **2** 70 marbles **3** 50 balls

Page 51

4 240 points **5** 22 stamps **6** 76 miles

Adding three 1-digit numbers

Page 52

1 18, 15, 14, 18 **2** 17, 12, 13, 16

3 Accept any correct addition calculations using the numbers provided

Page 53

4 14, 9, 20

5

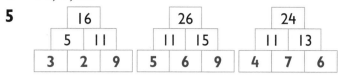

6 5, 6, 5, 7, 6, 9, 8, 9, 4

Two-step problems

Page 54

1 24 players **2** 32 books **3** 13 people

Page 55

4 126 planks of wood

5 £31

6 11 apples

Commutativity

Page 56

1 For each question, accept the three numbers rearranged in two different ways, e.g. 7 + 8 + 5, 5 + 7 + 8, 5 + 8 + 7, 8 + 5 + 7 or 8 + 7 + 5

2 17, 8 and 17, 8, 3 and 8, 12, 4 and 12

3 8, 9

Page 57

4 24 − 6 = 18 and 24 − 18 = 6
33 − 9 = 24 and 33 − 24 = 9

5 15 + 25 = 40, 25 + 15 = 40, 40 − 15 = 25 and 40 − 25 = 15
27 + 22 = 49, 22 + 27 = 49, 49 − 22 = 27 and 49 − 27 = 22

6 86, 53 + 33 = 86, 86 − 53 = 33 and 86 − 33 = 53
86, 39 + 47 = 86, 86 − 39 = 47, 86 − 47 = 39

Addition and subtraction within 100

Page 58

1 60, 80, 40

2 50, 30, 70, 30, 10, 60

3 70, 90, 100, 80, 90, 90, 70, 50, 80, 90, 50

Page 59

4 41, 63, 96, 57, 74, 86

5 21, 41, 71, 31, 51, 61, 23, 45, 78, 39, 56, 68

6 45, 64, 49, 82, 68, 88

Check your progress

- Shade in the stars on the progress certificate to show how much you did. Shade one star for every ⭐ you circled in this book.
- If you have shaded fewer than 20 stars go back to the pages where you circled Some ☆ or Most ⭐ and try those pages again.
- If you have shaded 20 or more stars, well done!

Addition and subtraction
Progress certificate

name _____ date _____

pages 4–5	pages 6–7	pages 8–9	pages 10–11	pages 12–13	pages 14–15	pages 16–17	pages 18–19	pages 20–21
1	2	3	4	5	6	7	8	9

pages 22–23	pages 24–25	pages 26–27	pages 28–29	pages 30–31	pages 32–33	pages 34–35	pages 36–37	pages 38–39
10	11	12	13	14	15	16	17	18

pages 40–41	pages 42–43	pages 44–45	pages 46–47	pages 48–49	pages 50–51	pages 52–53	pages 54–55	pages 56–57
19	20	21	22	23	24	25	26	27

Did you find all 26 mice?

(Including this one!)

pages 58–59
28